# Beating the Heat, Desert Style

## by Ja

HOUGHTO

D1379136

BOSTON

The Living Desert Botanical Gardens, in Palm Desert, California

**W**hen you picture a desert, do you see a camel crossing miles of sand dunes? Such deserts do exist, but sand dunes make up less than twenty percent of the world's desert areas. Other deserts around the world are known for salty lakes, tall mountains, strangely shaped rocks, or even year-round ice and snow.

In the deserts of the American Southwest, you can find grasslands, waterfalls, rivers, and streams, as well as many plant and animal species, some of which are not found anywhere else in the world. But the Southwest is like all desert environments in one important way: the living things that survive there get by with less than ten inches of precipitation, in the form of rain or snow, each year.

How do Southwestern plants and animals survive with so little water? Often they rely on the same strategies that David Alloway, a desert-survival trainer, teaches people to use. For example, Alloway warns his students to move around as little as possible when the sun's rays are beating down the strongest. Desert creatures like the gila [HEE-luh] monster, rattlesnake, and porcupine use this strategy.

Most desert animals come out only early in the morning, at dusk, or after sundown to find food. Some animals, like

Pocket gopher

pocket gophers, rarely come out at all. Underground, where they live, they seek out roots of tasty plants. Then they pull on the roots until the plants drop down to their cool burrows.

Even diurnal [dy-UR-nuhl] creatures—those that come out during the day, such as the kingbird and desert iguana [ih-GWAH-nuh]—renew themselves by taking an occasional nap in the hottest part of the day. Other desert animals, like the round-tailed ground squirrel and the spadefoot toad, estivate, or sleep all summer, much the way bears in cold climates hibernate, or sleep all winter.

The seasons in the Southwestern desert are different from those in milder climates. Most naturalists agree that the desert has five seasons. Rainfall affects the timing and character of every season, and in the desert the rain is unpredictable. The desert spring lasts from February until April. Next comes the foresummer, or dry summer, in May and June. The summer monsoon falls from July to mid-September, when tropical winds bring brief but violent thunderstorms. Autumn lasts from late September until November, and winter rounds out the year in December and January.

Birds that can't tolerate the heat follow cycles set by the seasons. They migrate to the Southwest during the cooler desert winters, then head north again when the weather gets too warm. These "snowbirds" include red-shafted flickers and sage thrashers.

Saguaro cacti (left) and desert paintbrush (right)

Of course, desert trees and plants can't just move to a shady area to get away from the hot sun, the way people and animals can. Plants have developed their own methods to beat the heat. The seedlings of the saguaro [suh-GWAHR-oh] cactus, which bears Arizona's state flower, often take root in the shadow of a mountain. Or they may grow beneath the shady shelter of a "nurse" tree or bush, like a mesquite [meh-SKEET]. And, like other night bloomers, the saguaro cactus waits to open its blossoms until after the sun sets.

Other plants and flowers, like the desert lily, behave like the animals that take a long nap during hot or cold weather. These plants survive by becoming dormant, or totally inactive, when they are deprived of water for a long time. When water again becomes available, they resume their activity.

Then there are fast-fading ephemerals [ih-FEHM-ur-uhlz] —plants that wait, sometimes years, for a heavy rainfall before they flower. These plants, such as desert paintbrush and Mojave [moh-HAH-vay] aster, live mostly in seed form, bloom for a few weeks, produce new seeds, and die soon after flowering. According to experts, there are literally hundreds of varieties of ephemerals in the deserts of the American Southwest.

When David Alloway takes kids hiking in the desert to see the miracles of nature, he advises them always to stay with the group. That way, there is less chance

Bat

of getting lost, and more chance of getting help fast if an accident happens. Desert animals also find safety in numbers. Creatures like honey ants, bighorn sheep, and many species of bats rarely live, travel, hunt, or work alone.

Alloway also insists that his students wear brightly colored clothing. This makes them easier to find if they should get separated from the group. Creatures like mule deer, coyotes, and rattlesnakes don't worry about being separated from their groups, though. They are more afraid of being seen by predators or prey. Nature protects these creatures by camouflaging them in earth colors, to make them more difficult for other animals to spot.

Coyote

Earth colors help desert animals in another way, too. Because these colors tend to be pale, they reflect sunlight, keeping the animals cooler than dark colors would.

But desert creatures are protected by more than their colors. They have fast feet, sharp claws, dangerous quills, or tough shells to help shield them from harsh weather and predators. Since people don't have this added protection, David Alloway insists that his students wear hats, boots, long-sleeved shirts, and long pants.

Alloway points out that this is how people who live in the desert dress. "They wear light-colored loose-fitting clothes, but they're completely covered, right up to their head and their necks," he says. This helps to protect the skin from the sun but allows air to flow through the cloth and cool down the body. A wide-brimmed hat provides shade and prevents the brain from overheating. The brain is "the best survival tool we have," according to Alloway.

Rattlesnake

"Despite the fact that people have moved on to many other areas of the globe, the human race is well adapted to the desert," asserts Alloway. Moreover, walking on two legs is a great advantage that humans have over four-legged animals. In a standing position, more of the body is exposed to cooling breezes, and the hands are free to work and carry objects. In addition, humans' smaller amount of body hair helps their skin stay cool.

As you might guess, Alloway's students pack plenty of water before heading into the wild. In the desert, it is more important to have water than food. Alloway says that most people already have a three-week supply of food energy stored up in fat, but they need at least a gallon of water per day. An adequate amount of water helps people think clearly and maintains the normal processes of the body's cells.

Some desert creatures have easy ways of carrying water along with them. Desert tortoises, for example, store water in their bladder, a trick that allows them to go a year or longer without taking a drink!

Animals that lack a built-in water jug have other mechanisms to help them adjust to the arid climate. Kangaroo rats convert their diet of dry seeds into fluid. They can go their entire lives without swallowing a single drop of liquid. Gila monsters and geckos [GEHK-ohz] have short, thick tails that contain fat, which helps them survive for long periods when no water can be found. A camel's hump also stores up fat, not water, for an emergency energy source.

Gila monster

Desert tortoise

11

Numerous desert plants also find ways to quench their thirst, or make do without water. Some, like the mesquite and the desert willow, develop very long roots that act like straws, helping them to suck up water from as deep as fifty feet or more below ground.

Some plants are parasites, living off the root system of another "host" plant. One of these plants, called sand food, lives below the sand and has a thick stem up to six feet long that attaches to the roots of nearby shrubs. It absorbs both nutrients from the host plant and water from the sand. A small, sand-colored flower is the only part of the plant that appears above ground. In the 1930s, 106 sand food plants weighing a total of forty-six pounds were found attached to a single host plant that weighed only one pound!

Other desert plants, including all cacti, are known as succulents—plants that store water in their roots, stems, or leaves. They replenish their water supply during the rainy seasons and thrive in hot temperatures.

This doesn't mean, though, that you can simply suck on a cactus to quench your thirst in the desert. Getting the juice from a cactus is hard and risky work, David Alloway warns, and it's not usually worth the effort. Cacti have spines or thorns that can be very painful. Some desert animals—such as the pig-like javelina [hah-vuh-LEE-nuh], with a tough, leathery snout, and the desert tortoise, with a sharp beak—have features that enable them to reach the tasty fruit of the prickly pear cactus without getting pricked. But some cacti have more than spines to protect themselves from hungry or thirsty creatures. Most cactus fruits and other wild plant foods contain acids that make people and animals sick. So unless you are an expert, never turn to a cactus for a refreshing desert drink!

Flowering mound cactus (far left) and javelina (near left)

Of course, not all the adaptations that desert plants and animals have made can be imitated by humans. Most types of desert wildlife have developed traits or behaviors that are distinctly their own. Reptiles, for example, like the desert tortoise, reabsorb water from their bodies. Jackrabbits have oversized ears that act like built-in air conditioners, releasing heat to help cool them. Many desert rodents drool all over their fur to bring down their body temperature when they get too warm. Vultures have the ability to fly high into the cooler breezes of the upper air during the midday heat.

Nature clearly has figured out a variety of ways to help wildlife flourish in the desert. There are probably as many different desert plant and animal adaptations as there are living things. David Alloway tells people that if they ever find themselves lost in the desert, the single rule to remember is this: Stay cool, and keep your cool. If people do this, they can most fully enjoy studying the life forms that make the desert landscape fascinating.

Turkey vulture

The dry climate of the Southwestern desert may not seem to support much life at first. But what looks like a harsh environment on the surface contains a wide variety of life forms in a system that is amazingly complex. Every living thing has a purpose, and desert wildlife has adapted to survive as a whole.

There is a saying about wild places that is especially true for the Southwestern desert: "Take only memories and leave only footprints." Wildlife in the American Southwest is persistent, but its habitat is fragile. People can learn how to survive in the desert by borrowing the ways that animals and plants have adapted to their environment. In return, however, people can give something back to the desert wildlife by helping to protect it.

Dune evening primrose